ON THE
ROAD

BEGINNING READER

LEVEL 1

50-250 WORDS

ON THE
ROAD

Wade Cooper

Cartwheel
·B·O·O·K·S· ®

SCHOLASTIC INC.

New York   Toronto   London   Auckland   Sydney
Mexico City   New Delhi   Hong Kong   Buenos Aires

What can you see
on the busy roads?
Cars, trucks, and buses
and tractors with loads.

All moving along,
some fast and some slow.
Do you know what they do?
Do you know where they go?

Copyright © 2008 make believe ideas ltd.

ISBN-13: 978-0-545-09994-3
ISBN-10: 0-545-09994-3
10 9 8 7 6 5 4 3 2 1   9 10 11 12 13
Printed in China
This edition first printing, January 2009

Reading together

This book is an ideal first reader for your child, combining simple words and sentences with stunning color photography of real-life cars, buses, tractors, and trucks. Here are some of the many ways you can help your child take those first steps in reading. Encourage your child to:

- Look at and explore the detail in the pictures.

- Sound out the letters in each word.

- Read and repeat each short sentence.

Look at the pictures

Make the most of each page by talking about the pictures and spotting key words. Here are some questions you can use to discuss each page as you go along:

- Why do you like this picture?

- What noise does this vehicle make?

- What kind of wheels does it have?

- What job does it do?

Look at rhymes

Some of the sentences in this book are simple rhymes. Encourage your child to recognize rhyming words. Try asking the following questions:

- What does this word say?

- Can you find a word that rhymes with it?

- Look at the ending of two words that rhyme. Are they spelled the same? For example, "roads" and "loads," and "go" and "slow."

Test understanding

It is one thing to understand the meaning of individual words, but you need to check that your child understands the facts in the text.

- Play "spot the obvious mistake." Read the text as your child looks at the words with you, but make an obvious mistake to see if he or she has understood. Ask your child to correct you and provide the right word.

- After reading the facts, shut the book and make up questions to ask your child.

- Ask your child whether a fact is true or false.

- Provide your child with three answers to a question and ask him or her to pick the correct one.

Quiz pages

At the end of the book there is a simple quiz. Ask the questions and see if your child can remember the right answers from the text. If not, encourage him or her to look up the answers.

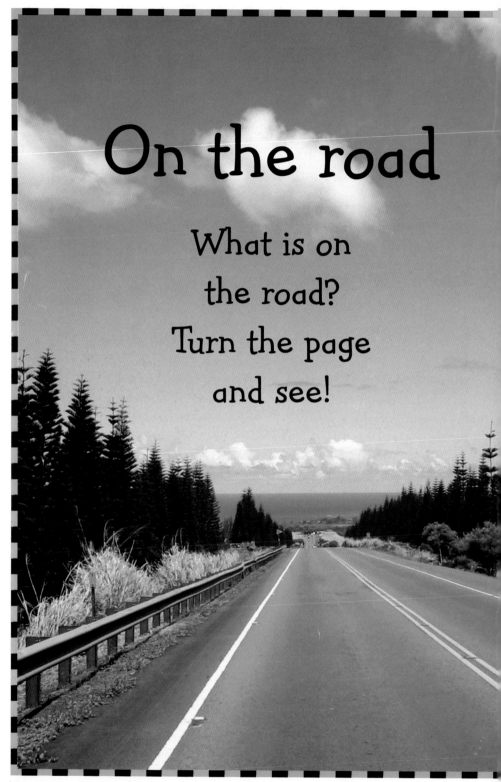

On the road

What is on
the road?
Turn the page
and see!

The engine in
this yellow car
makes it go –
fast and far.

Go, go, go!
Don't be slow.

Beep
Beep

They roll along
on busy roads.

Honk

Trucks pull
many kinds
of loads.

Honk

cab

radiator

wheel

exhaust

I'm a mixer.
Here I come.
I mix concrete
in my big drum!

Mix

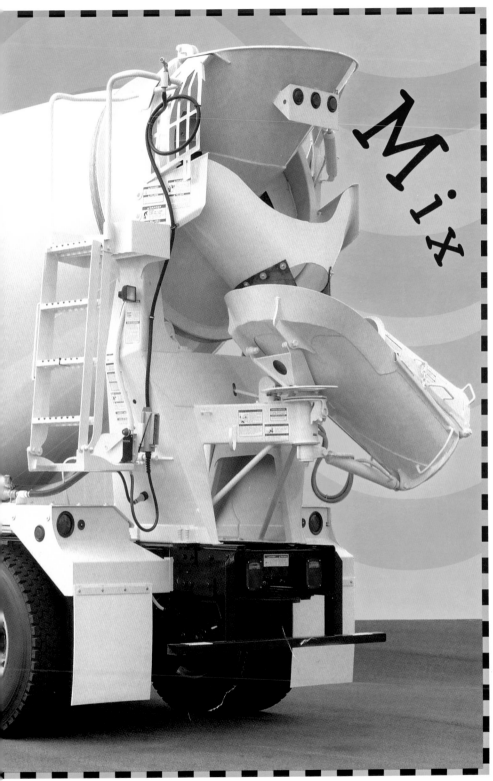

Mix

Fire truck

ladder

wheel

equipment

lights

Whee-woo. Whee-woo! Whee-woo!

"Fire! Fire!"
the people shout.

Here comes a fire truck
to put the flames out.

My arm is long.
My bucket is big.
I was made to
dig, dig, dig!

Dig

Dig

Woo-Woo
Woo-Woo!

Hear my siren.
I'm on the way.

I will come
to save the day.

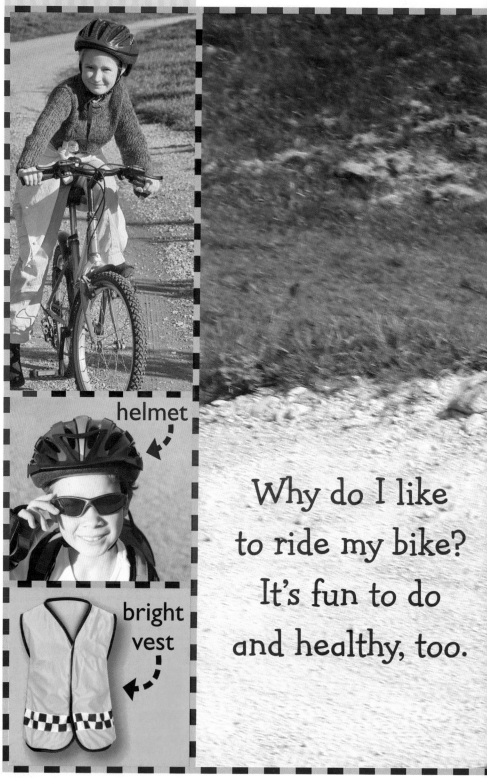

Bicycle

helmet

bright vest

Why do I like to ride my bike? It's fun to do and healthy, too.

Bring-bring!
Bring-bring!

A motorbike
is fun to ride
through the pretty
countryside.

Vroom! Vroom!

It's the big yellow bus
to take us to school.

SCHOOL BUS

All aboard! Move down!
Let's go! Keep cool!

I pull plows and
heavy loads
on grassy fields
and muddy roads.

What do

1. What makes cars go fast?

The engine.

2. What should you wear when you ride a bike?

A helmet and a bright vest.

3. What do tractors pull?

Plows and heavy loads.

you know?

4. Which truck goes
to put out fires?

The fire truck.

5. How do you know the
ambulance is coming?

You can hear the siren.

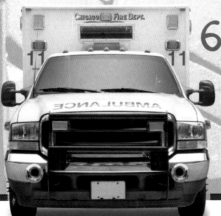

6. What color is
the school bus?

Yellow.

Useful words

engine
An engine is a machine that uses fuel to make things move.

plow
A plow is a heavy farm tool that turns the soil. It is pulled along by a tractor.

helmet
Always wear a helmet when you ride a bike.

shout
When you shout, you speak loudly.

healthy
Healthy things are good for you.

ook • we • like • and •

key words

Here are some key words used i
Make simple sentences for the other words
in the border.

Cars **go** fast.

This is a cement
truck. **It** mixes
concrete.

Tractors work **on** grassy
fields and muddy
roads.

Here **comes** the fire truck.

Diggers have a
big bucket.

the • was • big • my • went • no • to • all •

Dear Family and Friends of New Readers,

Welcome to Scholastic Reader. We have taken more than eighty years of experience with teachers, parents, and children and put it into a program that is designed to match your child's interest and skills. Each Scholastic Reader is designed to support your child's efforts to learn how to read at every age and every stage.

- First Reader
- Preschool - Kindergarten
- ABC's
- First words

- Beginning Reader
- Preschool - Grade 1
- Sight words
- Words to sound out
- Simple sentences

- Developing Reader
- Grades 1 – 2
- New vocabulary
- Longer sentences

- Growing Reader
- Grades 1 – 3
- Reading for inspiration and information

On the back of every book, we have indicated the grade level, guided reading level, Lexile® level, and word count. You can use this information to find a book that is a good fit for your child.

For ideas about sharing books with your new reader, please visit www.scholastic.com. Enjoy helping your child learn to read and love to read!

Happy Reading!

—Francie Alexander
Chief Academic Officer
Scholastic Inc.

I pull plows and
heavy loads
on grassy fields
and muddy roads.

FIRST READER
LEVEL PRE 1
30-100 WORDS

ABC's &
first words.

BEGINNING READER
LEVEL 1
50-250 WORDS

Sight words,
words to sound
out & simple
sentences.

DEVELOPING READER
LEVEL 2
250-750 WORDS

New vocabulary
& longer
sentences.

GROWING READER
LEVEL 3
700-1500 WORDS

Reading for
inspiration &
information.

Based on the best research about how children learn to read, Scholastic Readers are developed under the supervision of reading experts and are educator approved.

"Scholastic Readers are designed to support your child's efforts to learn how to read at every age and every stage. Enjoy helping your child learn to read and love to read."

Francie Alexander
CHIEF ACADEMIC OFFICER
SCHOLASTIC INC.

BEGINNING READER	GRADE LEVEL	GUIDED READING LEVEL	LEXILE® LEVEL	WORD COUNT
Level 1	Pre-K–1	F	190L	151

For more information about Scholastic Readers visit www.scholastic.com

$3.99 US / $4.50 CAN

ISBN-13: 978-0-545-09994-3
ISBN-10: 0-545-09994-3

Cartwheel
·B·O·O·K·S·®

an imprint of

■SCHOLASTIC

www.scholastic.com

50399

EAN

9 780545 099943

Singer Sewing Library: Short Cuts to Home Sewing, How to Make Dresses and How to Make Children's Clothes

Singer Sewing Machine Company